ON THE EDGE OF AN ISLAND

Work by Jean 'Binta' Breeze

BOOKS

Riddym Ravings (Race Today, 1988)
Spring Cleaning (Virago, 1992)
On the Edge of an Island (Bloodaxe Books, 1997)

RECORDINGS

Tracks, album with Dennis Bovell Dub Band
(LKJ Records, 1991)
Riding on de Riddym: Selected SpokenWorks, cassette
(57 Productions, 1997)*

* This 60-minute cassette features 30 poems from Jean 'Binta' Breeze's books and performances, including *On the Edge of an Island*. Available from 57 Productions, 57 Effingham Road, Lee Green, London SE12 8NT, price £6.95 (ISBN 1 899021 01 9).

ON THE EDGE OF
AN ISLAND

JEAN 'BINTA' BREEZE

BLOODAXE BOOKS

ISBN: 1 85224 405 4

First published 1997 by
Bloodaxe Books Ltd,
P.O. Box 1SN,
Newcastle upon Tyne NE99 1SN.

Bloodaxe Books Ltd acknowledges
the financial assistance of Northern Arts.

Cover printing by J. Thomson Colour Printers Ltd, Glasgow.

Printed in Great Britain by
Cromwell Press Ltd, Broughton Gifford, Melksham, Wiltshire.

*For the people of Hanover, Jamaica,
and in memory of my grandfather, Papa Basie.
These are stories of the present, not the past
from somewhere behind God's back
as we would say in Jamaica.*

Acknowledgements

Acknowledgements are due to Serpent's Tail and 57 Productions who first published some of the work in this book. 'Cousin Eva' appeared as 'A Little Piece of Land, Lord' in *Sacred Space*, edited by Marsha Rowe (Serpent's Tail, 1993). 'Call Her Judas' was included in a Serpent's Tail cassette and Channel 4 film, both called *Short Stories for Long Nights* (1992). 'Grandfather's Dreams', 'caribbean woman' and 'one last dub' are read by Jean 'Binta' Breeze on the cassette *Riding on de Riddym: Selected Spoken Works* (57 Productions, 1997).

Thanks are also due to Carolyn Cooper for her invaluable help.

Contents

9   I Will Come

12   Grandfather's Dreams

15   Old Day Passing

20   Maroon song

22   'tek a trip from Kingston to Jamaica'

24   Easter Lilies

31   grass

32   Widow

33   Cousin Eva

38   Homegrown

42   for Bertha

43   Talking Gospel

47   Mothersong

49   pipe woman

50   Call Her Judas

54   mansong

55   Porty

60   packing

61   today

62   Sunday Cricket

67   Song for Lara

70   caribbean woman

74   Kitchen Talk

78   one last dub

80   The Last Temptation

83   Ratoon

86   Return

91   I Jonah

I Will Come
(blues song to a muse, from exile)

somehow I thought you'd like to know
what happens here without you
tried in every way to show
just how I felt about you
although it seems you're always here
there's a space just waiting for you
it's not so bad in daylight
evening's full of silences

will you come tomorrow, will you come

lay last night dreaming
through a skylight

woke up screaming
someone took my voice

grabbed myself, terrified
listened for a song
but someone's taken my hearing now
I'm feeling I'm all wrong

somehow I thought you'd like to know
what happens here without you
tried in every way to show
just how I felt about you
although it seems you're always here
there's a space just waiting for you
it's not so bad in daylight
evening's full of silences

will you come, tomorrow, will you come

jumped up
full of dreading
tried the coffee break
mongst the pen and paper
scheduled for my verse
but something came at midnight
and left with all my words

    got dressed
    went out hunting
    fireful and tense
    mind distraught
    by what was left
    a bitter twisted sense

somehow I thought you'd like to know
what happens here without you
tried in every way to show
just how I felt about you
although it seems you're always here
there's a space just waiting for you
it's not so bad in daylight
evening's full of silences

will you come, tomorrow, will you come

tracked tears into corners
squeezed out rancid truth
if you will be my Moses
I will be your Ruth
picked my voice up gently
tested it for range
echoing through the midnight
from belly to the moon
found you waiting for me
by a river, by a sea
heard your gentle pleading
'home to me...home to me'

somehow I thought you'd like to know
what happens here without you
tried in every way to show
just how I felt about you
although it seems you're always here
there's a place just waiting for you
it's not so bad in daylight
evening's full of silences

I will come, with morning, I will come

Grandfather's Dreams

His hands were
working hands
spread out on the table
they became maps
veined roads
intertwining
everything was touched
with care
these hands would free
the unseen shoots
of soft green baby leaves
would carve out land
for yams
like African sculptures
would beat time rhythmic
checking breadfruits
ready for the eating
would
in the simple doing of a task
show us all our crafting
all our art

and his eyes
his vision
held somewhere in the heavens
were like clouds
promising us
growing up on rock
much needed rain

he sat lightly
on his clay mountain
where the sun
blackbronzed his face
into golden masks of ancestors

shapes and colours changing
with each new hour of the day

the cinnamon steam
of chocolate mornings
cooled
in his coco podded hands
the midday oilsheen sweat
he wiped away
the evening coal-black cool
of his homecoming
smelling of bush
and ripening naseberries
feeding the birds he knew as well as
neighbouring families

and when the winds
drifted us
overseas
in search of dreams
in search of 'tings gettin betta'
because we could not swim to Africa
and when we did not find the
gold he never sought
just   more horizons
like he'd known, somehow,
that people do the same things everywhere
how many of us
drowned in desperate ways
Atlantic drinking in our cries
how many of us
hands now bloodied
in the factory's making
of shapes we did not dream
find our hands
with or without our knowledge
reaching for
a straw

some clay
a metal scrap
some words
to shape a moment richer
than anything we sought
and in the making
see him
pause
and look for us
over more than distance
more than time

and we
holding something sacred
in our hands
hands now mapped
from other journeys
veined with newer songs
would reach out
place it on his mantle
knowing it cost
some million heartbeat
and say
'Asante sana baba'

this is
for you

Old Day Passing

Every few miles along the winding country road, you come across a square just like this one...sleeping in the dirt and heat. Each building has the same reddish brown colour where the soil, brushed on by wind and rain, covers the stripped and faded tints of undercoats that mark past moments of surplus, now dried out in the sun.

The dog, lying in the middle of the road, had seemed dead. Now it stirred with the passing car and, lazily scratching skin and bone, moved slowly to the large stone step that led into the shop. The car, changing gear down one to meet the hill, shook the dust for a moment, shifted the history of the landscape, then disappeared while its sound hung on.

The shop, unmoved, was the only one still open. Across the road two others were boarded up, the fading Wray and Nephew rum signs barely readable, old political slogans worn down to odd letters.

The dog, now trying to slink unnoticed round the corner of the top step into the shop, was met by a hard push from a foot clothed in an old waterboot which looked like the same dog had eaten it off at the top. Tucked halfway into the boot was the ragged end of worn out khaki trousers.

Faithful servant, ever humble, pulled back into the shade at the corner of the steps, curled up again, this time studying a lone fly intent on pitching in the dark circle of some sticky unknown thrown out through the window by one of the two men sitting in the gloom inside.

'Dat look like Miss Hilda son gawn up again. Ah hear she sickly.'

'Ai! Is not only ole tree Gilbert shake up. Mi black suit never wear so often as in de laas two months.'

There was a long memoried silence as both men contemplated storms, Gilbert, the most recent. Their eyes drifted through the window over the fallen giant of the old guango tree and the new ferns now nestling in new-found light.

Never to rise again, old hero, never to rise again.

They sat there, wrapped in old smells...kerosene and pickled mackerel, flour married to washing soap and...striking through, the immediate knife of J.B. rare, the rank sweet rum.

The man behind the counter looked anything but Jolly, yet that had been the family name for generations. He reached down slowly under the counter for a stained damp rag and, lifting each glass, wiped the curling linoleum cover clean, a ritual sense that needed no dirt.

A flask, half full, stood between them and their glasses. It was their point of focus between swigs of conversation.

'Yuh hear fram yuh daughter?'

'Yes. Ah get a letter wid some money a couple weeks ago. She couldn' come out after de storm troo she didn' have her right papers an dem wouldn' let her back een.'

'Betta she stay den.'

'Dat's right! Ah write an tell her dat even if ah dead, yes sah, even if ah dead, it betta she stay an get de papers.'

Nothing rose out of his face but his voice as his swollen fingers curled around the glass, giving it weight. He decisively raised it, and, as if swallowing a slice of life, wrinkled his face in pure distaste. His belly, holding on to the water, opened his mouth to belch out the fire.

'Beg pardon.'

The bartender, now shopkeeper, turned to arrange some of the few items left on one corner of the near empty shelves... sardines...three tins of cocoa...half a dozen bottles of aerated water...

'Goods truck late today.'

'Ah hear de radio man sey dat war bruk out in town, so maybe nutting moving.'

'Is really de saalfish ah hopin dem bring dis week an some chicken parts. People can always fine a piece a yam but all de banana an breadfruit down so ah sellin nuff flour an rice. But de meatkind, cyaan buy enuff to sell.'

'Look how tings did plentiful an cheap eena fi we days eh?'

'Ai, bwoy, is develop dem say we develop now.'

'Develop! dat jus mean every one pack up an gawn, dat is all de develop I see.'

'Like a whole generation missing.'

'Beg yuh move back a likkle mek a open dis door wider… an pull up de side shutter fi me. Ah don' want de truck fly paas an tink we shut.'

They both eased themselves slowly into action, knowing their bones well and accommodating any pain. They knew their pain like they knew each other, and quenched the worst of it with the heat of rum.

Holding the shutter open with a length of wood now smooth with time, he stood, held in a shaft of sunlight with dust specks floating round him like atoms of some distant universe, a relic. The bartender pulled the doors back wide onto the empty square then moved back round behind the counter squeezing his belly through the narrow opening.

Pulling themselves back on to their stools, the last two drinks were poured out of the flask. Now it was empty, they both looked through the window, eyes shuttered from the glare. One could not afford to buy another round and one could not afford to give it free.

The land opposite stared back at them silently, lying flat all the way out to where a ridge of roseapple showed the path of the river and beyond that to the distant hills.

Again a moment held and treasured, buried deep, unspoken. Time released them with a sigh and they turned, picked up their glasses and, as if from lessons learnt the hard way, measured their swallows.

'Tink we'll ever see dem lan full up wid crop again de way it was wen we was bwoy?'

'None a Busha pickney nat comin back here to farm. De ole house on de hill, it rotten, gawn to nutten.'

'Good lan like dat jus lie dung idle. Yuh tink dem rememba sey dem own it?'

'Dem nuh rememba now, but mek one a we jus start buil someting ova dere an yuh see how faas dem rememba.'

'Well, me wouldn' spen my energy pon a nex man lan.'

'Neida mi!'

The view became too much and they drew their eyes back in, only to face the empty bottle.

'Sell mi one sheet a airpaper an one airmail envelope.'

The bartender/shopkeeper wiped his hands on the khaki apron hanging from under his waist and shuffled carefully past the pickled barrels to the distant shelf where delicate landless dreams were held. Carefully, he took down a pad of writing paper and tore one out, then took an envelope from a pack, the small square of red, white and blue seeming trivial in his hand. Returning to the counter he tore a piece of brown wrapping paper and folded it round them to protect from any touch of the hard brownred dirt that might make them real. He handed them across into the overworked criss cross of swollen veins and fingernails like bones, where words were held like heavy stones.

Together, they picked up their glasses, and this time, swallowing quickly, a final putting down.

'Walking out dis evening?'

'If de good Lord spare.'

He reached into the corner of the door for his felt hat, sat firmly on his stick. Both had grown old with him, one knew his head, one knew his hand and altogether, they knew this land and how to make room for a slip of paper. At home, it would be folded and placed inside the big flat bible by his bedside table until he could work out a way to weigh words, choosing the best, carefully, like yams for market. The rest he'd learnt to eat himself.

Leaving the bartender washing out the flask to use again and putting the glasses to soak in a bucket of suds under the counter, he took his first steps down.

Walking home, slowly and carefully on the dusty whiteglare rock of road, the dog slinking in curves behind him, he suddenly felt tired and eased himself onto the banking, sitting for a moment in the shade of the last limb left on the big mango tree that marked the end of Busha's land.

He fell asleep, hat over his eyes, the stick laid out beside him, a fly investigating the remains of sugar from the rum around his mouth. A while later, the dog licked his face and wandered home, leaving a handkerchief of red, white and blue paper making small attempts to fly with each passing touch of air.

The bartender got the news sometime later and, squeezing himself into his bedroom/storeroom at the back of the shop, took out his one black suit and searched the legs for signs of earth.

Last week's funeral had been in mud and rain.

Maroon song

rocky road
nuh frighten duppy
an cotton tree
have shade
so bwoy no tek no libaty
fah mi ready now fi dead

Bogle a mi uncle
an Nanny rule mi head
Quashie pass yah often
an Cuffy son nuh dead

so yuh sayin we mus satisfy
wid tings jus how dem is
wile yuh pop big style an prosper
an live ova we head

an jus because mi tell yuh
say mi nah go wuk fi dat
yuh spread it say mi lazy
an a gwaan like Big Sprat

mi pickney dem nuh hungry
fah mi plant eberyting
mi know seh if de shap lack
yuh whole tribe gwine go drap dung

dis yah likkle islan
kudda been a paradise
nat only jus fah touris
but people wid open eyes

yuh prefer fi bline we
You tief an say crime nuh pay
but fram de days of Henry Morgan
a robbery hold de sway

an mi weh hol' Independence
firmly in mi han
yuh waan come underrate an pay
like slavery pon de lan

dark night
nuh badda rolling calf
an red claat tie we head
so bwoy nuh tek no libaty
cause ah ready now fi dead

'tek a trip from Kingston to Jamaica'

so often, uncle,
yuh voice
come chanting true

sit mi dung pon rockstone
an tinking nuff tings troo

once de road from Cascade
to Kingston
was wid ease
but since de violence an ting
town become a squeeze

it hard fi look pon pikibo
all a Nanny children dem
katch up eena zinc fence
an a bun up eena sun
an de question of de lan
lef to de dying one

seem like revolution come an gawn
an revolutionary son
full im house fram merica
an talk like spida man

an de lan jus lie dung
haunted
by de spirits of we paas
fa de *fila* an de *nike*
no fi dutty up pon grass

ole plantation lie dung idle
an de coas, it running white
de mountain hard behin we
an de lan still rule by spite

'ah no we start it
mash it dung
wen dem come back een
mek dem buil it again'

see saw
marjorie daw
Jammy shall have a new master
he shall squat
just an acre a year
because he can't fence any faster

so long now, uncle
yuh did beg we
'no sell out'
fi tek we time an
come at fi we speed

but de red yeye ketch we
an fish barrel hold we dung
an freedom is a wud
dat twis we tongue

Easter Lilies

Max didn't really think much about it when he arrived back home mid afternoon and Uncle Massa wasn't there.

He had given Uncle Massa breakfast early as usual, a little bush mint tea, sweet the way he liked it and some hard-dough bread with steam callaloo cut from the patch behind the kitchen. He had then gone off himself to move the goats and put in a few hours cleaning through the bananas and weeding out the yams.

Then, as the midday sun started baking everything, he had pulled out the bundle of their clothes, stowed in the crutch of the guango tree, and made his way to the river. Using the last of his stock of cake soap which he kept hidden under a rock, Max washed the clothes, spreading them out on the grass to dry.

Then it was his turn.

He enjoyed this hour swimming in the Blue Hole. It was where he had learnt. As little boys they had dived off the bank above, the braver ones from the tree that grew there. It wasn't something to try in the dry season though, when there was only a trickling feed, as his cousin had found out when he hit a rock on the bottom and split his head open. Max was too old for such games now, but he alone, of all his generation, still roamed the same places, still knew the sweetest fruit trees, still bothered to replant anything that had died over the years.

Occasionally the others returned from foreign places with addresses made up of numbers and letters, returned with strange wives, husbands and new children. For a day or two they would try to impress their spouses with their ability to live in the wild. Then they would call Max to take them through the bush tracks, to take them to the river for a cookout, to climb and reach the high fruits for them, to protect their children from every kind of bite or accident possible, all the time slapping his back and congratulating him on choosing to stay and live the simple life, while being absolutely sure themselves that Max had to be more than a bit simple to choose to live that way, in these times.

They never stayed more than a couple of days before having to go and visit relatives in town, Montego Bay or Kingston, where there were indoor toilets and burglar bars, where the car could drive up to the front door and they could feel secure once more with their big bundle of keys. They had learnt to live now with no space and, certainly, no insects.

On leaving, they would walk behind Max, who would be loaded with food for them, out to where the track met the road and their rented car was parked. Calling out 'good mornings' to everyone they met, giving spare dollars to the wide-eyed children hiding halfway behind the bananas, while shaking the car keys in one pocket waiting to fit it into a lock. They were happy. They, at least, had remembered and returned. Many didn't. Couldn't! And hadn't they left Max all the shirts and pants they had that could fit him plus a few dollars change to 'buy a drink'.

After all, Max didn't want much. He was simple, just like Uncle Massa. Seemed like there was one in every generation.

They would then make their escape after one ritual rum in the same old bar with the ageing owner. One ritual rum to congratulate themselves on having escaped such poverty and boredom. One ritual rum to cover the fleeting fear of possible failure that might land them right back here. One ritual rum for their return tickets to wherever.

Enjoying the cool of the river, Max was thinking of his brother, the last one to have come. Delroy and his wife had convinced their mother to return with them to Canada to take care of their two young children. Apparently they couldn't afford someone there, no matter how much they earned.

He wished she hadn't gone. She, already looking so tired, had looked after so many grandchildren until her sons and daughters, abroad or in town, had earned enough to send for them. What was more, these last two had been born abroad and apparently had never been told that elders were people children should respect and listen to and certainly should not be kicked or screamed at for saying 'no' at times. He had known she wouldn't refuse, so she was now in Toronto, looking after two more.

And strangely, she had been glad to go, despite the leaving of her seasons, her fruit had been placed there for some reason that 'God only could tell'. Perhaps He knew a quarter acre couldn't feed that many. All her children and grandchildren were now overseas, all the family, except Max and Uncle Massa. No ambition. They had no ambition. Look how long she'd fought to make something of them, to push them out of the village so they wouldn't have to repeat what she'd done all her life. And the whispers that had clouded her eyes, swirling, halfway spoken, that maybe…'God help me'…maybe… they weren't…'not that word'…hadn't been…all man. It seemed certain that Max wouldn't give her any grandchildren. Who in their right mind want to take up with a young man who didn't intend going any further. Not in this day and age. And in the last few years, especially when the visitors came, she had found it increasingly difficult to smile at Max and Uncle Massa, especially Uncle Massa, whom she thought had led Max astray.

Uncle Massa didn't talk much, never had, but when he greeted you with a smile, you always had to wonder how someone could grow old with such innocence and beauty in his eyes. In the real world, it was easier to think him senile or even, retarded.

Max knew better. He had instinctively followed Uncle Massa as a child, much to the anger of his mother. His father hadn't had much to say about it simply because he wasn't there. He had emigrated to England when Max was a baby and had never returned or made contact since. Occasionally, others returning, would mention seeing him on the street corner in Birmingham or some such place. Max mostly heard about him when his mother, tired of the trouble from her sons, would blame him, saying they were just like him. Max soon learnt his own escape.

Dressed in his khaki uniform for school, he would go for a while in that general direction, then hide his books and take the track back to wait for Uncle Massa. He was sure from very early that the things he learnt from Uncle Massa were of the greatest importance...where all the different birds nested, special mango trees that were not common to the area, patches of clay that could be made into any shape and baked in the hot sun, where the biggest mountain crayfish could be caught under the cool stones in the river.

At first, Max was amazed how all the small animals would come to Uncle Massa, how the birds would fly into his hands, amazed, until they all accepted him too and he became a part of the magic of the land.

On the few days that his mother marched him all the way to school, he sat there, through the spelling, through the times tables, through the reading of stories about little lords in England, all the time itching to tell his stories, to share some of his secret moments, but teacher only ever asked that they repeat what had been said. Otherwise they had to learn bible verses and Max could never remember them at all...except one...about the lilies in the valley...and then he would gaze through the window and see the fresh burst of Easter lilies down by the river, miles away, in James Gully. Then, from his dream world, struggling over an answer to a question he hadn't heard, he would be put to stand in a corner holding on to one ear and one leg till he was cramped and the class was cramped with laughter.

Uncle Massa taught him to listen, not so much to words, but to all the sounds around him, until he could feel himself part of the heat, the earth, the trees, the sky, part of the universe.

Soon, the family had given up on Max, like they had given up on Uncle Massa many years before. They were glad at least that Max would work the land where Uncle Massa had simply lived with it. Max at least would bring food home. And now, despite faint tinges of guilt, wrapped up warm against the cold many miles away, they were thankful that someone was left back home to keep an eye on the quarter acre, the house and Uncle Massa, and that strangers hadn't taken over.

Max didn't start worrying until he had finished cooking dinner and was drawing the firesticks. He sat there for a while, waiting, and watching the grey ash on the dying coals.

The pot of soup hung over the fire, full of corn in coconut milk and green with injun kale. Uncle Massa didn't care too much for meat so Max planted grains and beans and as many vegetables as he could.

He sat there waiting. Uncle Massa's eyes were growing dim now and he didn't usually stay out after dark which fell swiftly, like death, making evenings short.

Lighting the bottle torch, Max headed up the track towards the square. It was Friday evening and by now most would have eaten, bathed and, dressed in foreign clothes from all their relatives, would make their way to this gathering point. The shop would stay open late, taking on the dual role of rum bar and would sell the most it had done for the week.

Friday evening was the laying off of khaki, the pasturing of donkeys and of work, the lighting of many lamps circling round the square, and the one electric light bulb standing naked in the moon, a sign they said, of things to come.

Ahead of him on the track, Max saw another light and could make out the voice of Fred calling out to the others 'line up de rum for Mento man a come!' Fred was the leading singer for the Mento sessions on a Friday and made the best rhumba boxes that spoke out the rhythmic basslines, in his spare time.

By the time Max reached the square, he had already begun setting up in front of Mass Bedda's shop and was knocking back his first shot of inspiration. Mass Bedda himself had pulled out his stool from behind the counter and was fixing the strings on his old banjo.

He had tried to teach Max to play many years ago, but Max had preferred to listen from somewhere across the valley where the music echoed in mellow tones and blended in with all his other sounds. It was the sore point with Mass Bedda though, how quickly the young men left the village, how much land that used to be heavy with crop now had no hands to tend it, and when his arthritis and the rum took hold of him, he wailed about who was going to play the banjo when he was gone. With the rain it was going to be a wailing night for sure as they all squeezed into the dry space by the bar and steamed.

Neither Mass Bedda, Fred, or anyone in the square had seen Uncle Massa. This wasn't surprising. Even in this small village people had developed a way of not seeing Uncle Massa or maybe it was Uncle Massa who had developed a way of not being seen. He wasn't necessary to anyone's existence or survival. No one needed to stop him to ask for extra cuttings of yam heads. He hadn't turned his hand to any trade or craft so he wouldn't be asked to fix a bed or drawer or make a cutlass or a knife. He had no children for them to complain about or any animals that might have eaten their crops. And he had been there so long, he was like an old song, so familiar, you never know it's playing in your head.

None of this bothered Max. He just didn't want Uncle Massa getting really wet and catching a bad cold. He knew his feet would lead him to all the favourite corners where a man could be silent with his gods. And so, torch in hand, he made his way down the other side of the mountain where he was sure that he had gone.

From the square above the bottle torch could be seen weaving through the trees like an overgrown peenie wallie as Max's voice called out in the high pitched hillside melody mingling with mento, lifting and curving with the land, ...'Uncle Massa ...Uncle Massa...'

As the night grew darker only crickets and treefrogs answered his call, playing like stick and fife parts on the steady beating drum inside his head. At the far scattered houses perched on tiny flats on the side of the mountain, dogs answered before their owners shouted a sleepy lack of knowledge. Late on into the night he took track after track, stopping once at a small wooden house to ask for a bit of that precious supply of kerosene to renew his torch. Still, only the night answered.

In a stand of mahoe near the stream, Patook the owl called and flew down to a nearer tree. The birds were awake here.

It was near dawn when he stumbled down a shale of rocks on the side of the river when the smell reached him and his childhood came seeping back. Only at this time of the year, at Easter, did that smell fill the valley, the smell of Easter lilies, a perfume of that moment, held between life and death.

Max knew where that first springing was. He followed the curve of the river, seeking it, the smell stronger, sweeter, erasing time and its markings, absorbing fear. Moving from rock to rock he rounded the corner to the first soft clutch of earth and there they were, flowering with the first light in the sky, covered with the tears of morning, and, curled round them, sleeping like a baby, his breath a rhythm, like the river, ...Uncle Massa.

As he felt Max near him, sure that he would come, he smiled.

'Everyting all right now...ah hold her troo de night...she pass troo safe...everyting all right now...don't worry bout a ting...see...er lilies spring...'

Max stood, rooted, his long locks hanging like vines from the branches on his head.

When the post office, two miles away, opened, after the weekend holiday, the telegram from Canada was delivered by bicycle to Max. Mass Bedda read it to him in a little gathering in the square.

'Mamma died on Friday night. Returning home for funeral. She wanted to be buried on her land.'

grass

from the rush of heated reason your calm
caught
my fury

slowly
you made evening
                    a place to be

            crosslegged
        on the carpet of our magic

Widow

She looks like
every crone or witch
you've ever seen

she talks
constantly
of relatives
and herbs
and times long gone

when her dreamtime mumma came
and granted her her wish
she
living in the sun
asked for sunshine
health
and strength

so
she lives here
the years root round her
she makes so much
a mite easier

He shades her eyes
with gladness

and she sings

this is not her book of life
this cover
where poverty paints
a woman
wizened
by the sun

Cousin Eva

> *One, two, tree, bwoy,*
> *mi an yuh a spree bwoy,*
> *come mek we pull togedda, bwoy...*

The chant went on and on, punctuated by the grunts of the men. Each time they got to the last line, they lifted the small wooden house on to the back of the truck.

Cousin Eva sat, her arms protecting a large wicker basket, the kind usually used to carry yams. It was covered with a clean tablecloth she had sewn herself from some white patterned material that Mass Beddie's daughter had given her last Christmas on a visit from America. Cousin Eva was very proud of that tablecloth. Every one had said it was good material for a church dress, but Cousin Eva knew she would look like a walking window. She had put in her neat blanket stitches all the way round the edge to keep it from fraying, peering over it in the evening light, her thimble glinting as her fingers moved. There had been a few small pieces left over which she had folded neatly and packed into one side of the basket for, God spare her life, she was going to make a frilly curtain for the window when the house was settled on the piece of land

> *One, two, tree, bwoy,*
> *mi an yuh a spree bwoy,*
> *come mek we pull togedda, bwoy.*

With a last gigantic lift, muscles straining, stomachs taut and glistening with sweat, the men finally eased the house off the concrete blocks which had been firmly pounded into the earth to support the house. It wasn't wise building a proper foundation until you were sure how long you could stay.

Cousin Eva had had her fill of family land. Her husband, Mass Abel, God bless his soul, had built their house on family land in James Gully, but when he passed on, his family had started all kinds of quarrel and argument about it. Since Mass Abel did not leave a title and Cousin Eva wasn't the warring kind, she had paid some men to move the house a little further up the road to a spot Mass Sonny was renting her.

Well, the little field of gungo that she planted each year, with a few yams to keep her going, was mashed down in the heavy rains two years ago. Last year the cows had run loose in her field and ruined the crop again. Mass Sonny wasn't much better off than her and needed the money for the land. There was nothing Cousin Eva could do but ask the church brothers to move her again.

That time she had been very hopeful. A distant cousin who owned a sizeable yam field, and did quite well rearing chickens, had offered her a house spot in exchange for weeding in the field and cooking for the men on work days. She had managed that for about a year before the arthritis had played up so bad, she couldn't manage climbing up and down the hills.

Cousin Eva wasn't the begging kind and, after all, you couldn't expect a man, cousin or not, to give you land for free, not in these times. She might be poor but she was brought up with her pride and not even arthritis was going to make her lose her dignity. So, she prayed hard and did what she could selling a little callaloo she grew in the back yard, knowing quite well that the Lord blessed those who helped themselves. Then, one day, Mass Sonny's pigs came in and rooted it all up. There was no one she could cry to but the Lord.

All through her tears she thought of Independence Day, the excitement in the village, and all the school children marching along the road with their new flags and the mugs that had been handed out with the emblem on the side. She still had hers, unused, in the cabinet. She had thought then that all the people without land would have been given a small piece and a title because, surely, independence meant owning your own land, but no, that didn't happen, and so she prayed again.

That time He really seemed to answer. A letter came to the Post Office from Mass Abel's one son in foreign land. He had stopped sending the regular postal order after Mass Abel died. No one could blame him for that. He wasn't Cousin Eva's son and had his own mother to take care of. She didn't have any children for Mass Abel, in fact, didn't have any children at all. Something, must be the Lord, pricked him to send the fifty pounds. She knew from the amount that she probably would never hear from him again. But, God bless his soul, he had remembered when she most needed it.

This time she decided to make a clean move and arranged a reasonable deal with Blue who drove the Bedward truck for the boss man. If you knew the driver well you could always make a deal on the side. It was how poor people got backra to work for them so they could take back a little for their own sweat and blood.

Cousin Eva knew that she had been a decent hardworking citizen all her life, and she wasn't, no Lord, she wasn't going to die in a poorhouse. If the government could pay to keep her there, then she was sure they wouldn't mind if she occupied a piece of government land. After all, if the government owned the land, then it belonged to the people. Cousin Eva was sure she was the people and was always thinking what a shame it was to see so much good land lying idle when so many people had none.

'*One, two, tree, bwoy*,' and the house was on the back of Blue's truck on its way to what was now called 'Capture Lan' in Cascade. Cousin Eva was sitting in her chair inside it, looking out the window, as they bounced along the country road for two miles or so.

She didn't know what put the thought in her mind, maybe she was getting stupid in her old age, but as they drove along, she couldn't help wishing that she could live in a house that kept moving, just like this. She could see a different sight everytime she looked out the window. That would be a good way to spend her last few years after living in one village for so long. After all, if you had to keep moving house so much, you could very well keep on moving, house and all. Still, that way, you couldn't plant anything. And so, thinking of growing new roots, she arrived on 'Capture Lan'.

One, two, tree, bwoy,
mi an yuh a spree bwoy,
come mek we pull togedda, bwoy.

The house was now firmly settled on new concrete blocks. As time passed, the foundations would be strengthened.

The men eased back, lifting caps, wiping brows. Surveying their work with pride, they smiled at each other in celebration of their strength and turned to Cousin Eva for the best part of the proceedings.

She already had the bottle of white rum out of the basket and was wiping the cups clean from any dust of travel. Cousin Eva wasn't a drinking woman but she had grown up with hardworking men and understood the need for a firey rum every now and then. She supposed Blue and the other men were a lot more regular, but they were good men.

Blue broke the seal of the bottle and poured a few drops in front of the door to the house.

'May de Lawd bless yuh, an yuh house!'

With deep belly laughs and slaps on each others' shoulders, the bottle was passed round, cup after cup refilling, until it was done.

Wiping away the grim expression that always comes with swallowing rum, Blue picked up Cousin Eva's basket and placed it ceremoniously inside the house. He could see the tears of thanksgiving in her eyes.

'Time to go back to Massa wuk.'

That evening as the moon rose, Cousin Eva watched it from her chair beside the window, her bible on her lap.

She reached a hand inside her bosom and pulled out a knotted handkerchief. Opening it out on the table, she separated the money into different piles. She knew what each was for. A good vegetable garden to eat from, she could sell the excess at the local market. Some chickens, and a fence to protect them, a good fence. She couldn't stand to lose another crop. Then, a good stove. She could bake and sell lunches to the children from the big school nearby.

Slowly bending, she removed her shoes. Favouring her right knee, she knelt by the chair.

'Tank yuh, Lord, tank yuh, a likkle piece a lan, tank yuh, Lord!'

She spent the whole night on her knees.

When the government notice came some two years later, she, and the others round her, were prepared to stand.

Homegrown

I

homegrown
never had full strength
but always there
stix
to tide you over

homegrown

didn't crash your brain
more like a gentle lover

homegrown
no hybrid grown
on dung
to make you run
for cover

homegrown
no transplanted tongue
selling out
over and over

homegrown
heads cut off
our native flower

homegrown
gift from a friend
homegrown
a whisper in the wind
homegrown
like a long lost limb
homegrown
searching the skies
for star-eyed children

II

in her mound
shaped like a rising
to a god
she gently pushes
stick
casts a dark eye
on the sun
and shutting one side
for rain
asks for bread

while cassavas sprout
her quick spear
through water
brings her
fish

now
in shingle
on the cast out shores
of cities
one last crippled note
inside her hand
she reaches over the counter
for wheat she does not grow
and fish
from Newfoundland

while
in the mountains
yam drums beat
down the soil to
cane sticks
bending backs to toil

her eyes search
the horizon

picturing greener
bucks
on the other side

but the canoe's days are over
this coast
will suck you in

a nervous spirit
trapped
between mountain and sea

cannot run fluid
across the sand
cannot catch crabs now
running
from the lobster legs
broiling in the sun

>   *'No more back bench*
>   *up front*
>   *to de edge of de bump*
>   *up front*
>   *to de edge of de bump.'*

gone to wind
this spirit
gone to wind
under a heavier pounding

dust from mortar rises
settling into clay

rise again
peaceful arawak
rise again

these drums of rage and fire
need a continent

III

that night
a star cried
and a baby
fell

for Bertha

Big Bertha
you don't look so fat no more
for years you settled with laughter
trashing eyes to tears
men fell round you
cushioned by largesse
   today you wear his grief
   fat worked off
   in heated kitchens

      this last one fell
        without a crutch

Talking Gospel

'Ah can imagine how yuh feel, mi dear, but just pray to de Lord, one day He might release her, open her eyes an mek her see. Oh Jesus, wen put yuh all into bringing dem up, eh mi dear, an try to prepare dem for a better life dan wat you did have. Look how she did do well eena domestic science eh, girl woulda get a decent husband dat would married her in de church, an she tek her lovely self gawn to live wid dat good fi nutten streggae bwoy, Lufus. Ah can imagine how yuh feeling, sister.'

Miss Libby's voice had a feel of tough cane edging teeth, but Sister Consy couldn't exactly ask her to leave the front verandah, or even begin to tell her the amount of work she was keeping her away from. No. For Miss Libby was a senior member of the church that Sister Consy just join and she had to be humble to the chosen voice of the Lord.

Still, she couldn't understand why there was always a feeling of malice when Miss Libby talk about anyone else in the village excepting her own two children.

Miss Libby's daughters were still at home with her, which explain why she could walk from one neighbour house to the other everyday, advising them on their family affairs. She knew what everybody's children, especially the girls, were doing, day and night, and had taken on the duty of reporting to the poor mothers and, as if that was not enough, suggesting what could be done to keep them in line.

Her own daughters had been kept so much in line that not one boy in the village had ever been considered good enough for them, either in their own minds or Miss Libby's. They were so well brought up. Right now they would be doing all the washing, ironing and cooking, leaving Miss Libby free to administer to the needs of the community.

She had gone as far as to start a group for women at the community centre, but so many quarrels had started from information gathered there that it had become unhealthy for most women to attend.

Miss Consy sighed as she thought of the big pan of clothes soaking in the back yard, waiting for her. She felt the pain start in her whitlow finger just thinking about it, but sick finger or not, they were going to be washed today. Miss Libby didn't have any boys so she didn't understand what dirty khaki could do to thoughts and hands. She didn't even dare to suggest that they go round back and talk while she worked. You didn't entertain Miss Libby anywhere but on the front verandah, not a senior member of the church, especially one who had been asked personally by God to keep an eye on the passersby.

Hearing the sigh, Miss Libby's voice mounted in sympathy, sounding a bit like Pastor's on Good Friday.

'The Lord see and know, Im see and know, these girls nowadays, yuh almost have to lock them in, not dat is their fault, but the boys in the district, no sooner they into long pants but they trying to bring sin into the girls dem mind, and if they would stop at the mind, it wouldn't be so bad. Ah had to watch and pray wid my two, ah telling yuh, watch and pray, and now they are a pride and example to the community.

Miss Consy knew full well that most of the young people couldn't stand the two girls. The one girl who had been married, had her husband so wrapped up that he couldn't stop and talk to any of his old school friends any more. Especially not since they'd convinced him to go and join the police force. None of the people in the village liked the police. They were an old fashioned people and thought anyone who would take an oath against his own mother should be avoided. Not Miss Libby though. Her daughters liked uniforms and there had been a lot of rumours about them when the soldiers had come to camp in the school grounds. Couldn't mention that to Miss Libby.

As the thought of the school grounds passed her mind, Miss Consy remembered the last girl's uniform and how she would have to go and search for a bit of thread she had hidden somewhere to stitch up the side that rip out last week. It was getting too small for the girl, but where was a new one to come from now? Things was hard since Cawpie take up and gone with neither a message or a sign.

That was what had finally sent her in search of the Lord. When she realised that she was left on her own after all these years of putting up with his rum drinking ways, left with six children between eight and nineteen, there was nowhere else she could think to go if she wasn't going to break down and give up the ghost altogether. It wasn't like she was still young enough to think of another man, so at least now, she wouldn't be a sinner any more.

She remembered when Pastor gave the altar call that day, and she found herself just bursting into tears and walking up to the pulpit, holding her bible tight. She had never turned back since then and Pastor had asked Miss Libby to keep in constant fellowship with her as a new soul.

It might be a sin to think so, but right now she could just go on round to her own little back yard and sing a chorus while she washed and she would feel much better. She didn't read half as well as Miss Libby, but she could pick out the words slowly, and she had already marked out the verses that gave her strength in her own bible so she could find them easy. She woke up again to Miss Libby's voice.

'But don't you fret, mi dear, the Lord will bring her to her senses and she will come right back home to you, where she belong.'

With all due respect to the workings of the Lord, Miss Consy prayed that Dulcie wouldn't have to come back, especially not with the young baby. Where was she going to put them, and how was the food going to stretch? Not that she could turn away her own child, but the boy wasn't really that bad. True, he didn't come near the church and had a tendency to follow sound system, but at least he had rented a room and put Dulcie and the baby and they were living together for all intents and purposes like man and wife. Where were two young people like them going to find money for a church wedding? It seemed much more sensible to her that they had saved a little money to buy a bed and a dresser and the baby was getting good milk feed. The boy had a trade, and when there was work in the area he passed early every morning. He wasn't a loafter, it was just the times.

45

Miss Consy knew quite well that you could set your hat too high and then can't reach it, and the way things were these days, it was better that you find your way little by little with someone coming from the same place as yourself. Far better than to run after one of the white shirt men that leave you as soon as they get a promotion and start to move with big company thinking that you weren't good enough any more. Especially after they can afford a helper to keep the white shirt clean. Then they start looking for a teacher or a nurse. Love didn't have much to do with it these days, and at least Dulcie and her boyfriend had been sweet since primary school. Yes Lord, all she hoped was that things worked out for them, no matter how slow the mill of the Lord might grind.

'Just pray to the Lord to put her back on the right track.' Miss Libby was rising, Miss Consy wringing her hands in both thanksgiving and pain.

'The day is so hot, you wouldn't have a little something to drink?' Miss Libby paused, looking into the clean, small room.

Miss Consy sighed again, trying not to feel ungrateful about the Lord's messenger. It was the last bit of sugar she was saving to mix with a lime and give to the children with some bread for supper.

Well, the Lord could never say He came to her thirsty and she didn't give Him to drink. She turned and walked into the hall, reaching for the one glass that didn't have a crack in it.

Mothersong

I

The lines are drawn
one for each child
there are seven now

past the point of hearing
belly screams
an somehow
Jah will provide

dis one a butcher
dat one a baker
an perhaps a sailor man wife

her feet spread out
clutching at clay
to carry more weight
the veins rise
   ugly

an de sugar, chile
de sugar

parson bless dem doah
every single one
for unlike de food
de prayer never done

II

in the school
the children sit
soon
it will be one hundred
to a class

but de man still saying
condum come
fi cut dung di black race
have yuh lot
spread out
skin out
an gi mi a son
but yuh nah go see mi
till di kingdom come

one a dem will gi yuh trouble
one a dem will gi yuh pain
but never mine yah chile
one a dem will ease de strain

the belly hangs now

doctor scrape it mah
not even good enuff fi manish water
an no adda way fi
bring de dinna come

in the school
children on the bench
chanting
Jack and Jill
went up the hill

later
they will add
their own endings

pipe woman

stripped down dry
and smoked

eyes like precious stones
inside the folding layers
of her skin

cheeks are sucked in
deep on a wooden stem

cup held
in wiry hands

fire enters
rolls around her tongue
fills her belly
   rope into knots
she turns a dark blue black
steams up
         an yuh can see rain coming

dancing clouds
leave the cavern of her mouth
her nose
        a sign of habitation

here
between battles
she breathes guidance

beware
if she bows to drink
for them
she belches fire

Call Her Judas

'Yuh no seet? Yuh no seet? Jesas Christ...tek it aff...it chokin mi...tek it aff...it chokin mi...'

The silence of the early Christmas morning was broken.

At first we thought it was the neighbouring children waking up with their fi-fis, but then the screams came again.

'Tek it aff...Jesas Christ Almighty Gaad...tek it aff..'

We rushed out.

There she was, dancing this crazy dance in the middle of the road. The egg boxes and bits of plastic bags that she had strung together for clothes were shaking round her making her a tribal dancer in the middle of some unseen fire.

The hot asphalt had no time to burn her feet. They never stopped long enough. Her scrawny fingers were tearing the skin from her neck in a frantic effort to remove whatever she felt there.

And her mouth. I could never forget her mouth, one dark cave in which her now almost black tongue fluttered like a trapped bat. There was so little left of her...so little.

And the people gathered on the street. And laughed.

But even in the coarseness of their laughter, you could hear the fright, the sure deep down knowledge that whatever had happened to her could happen to them too. Still, they laughed.

Suddenly, she seemed to fly, her jumps taking her high into the air, her landings bare and slight. The cords on her neck stretched and she plucked at them like a guitar player who had learnt to hate his instrument.

'Tek it aff...it chokin mi...tek it aff...'

A bus, coming down the road, slowed early from the sight of the gathering. It managed to pass her by sticking close to the grassy bank, the driver fearing that one leap would fling her to the wheels. He couldn't stop. This was not a sight for tourists. Even air-conditioned, behind sunglasses, their eyes popped out the windows, wondering if this was a native spectacle, a Christmas carnival. But in that moment's wondering, they too felt a twinge of fear.

One car, coming on too fast, screamed on bad brakes to a stop as, slowly, people gathered round her in the road. The driver and a few others also brought to a stop joined them thinking it must be a Christmas jonkunnu band.

She leapt into the air and landed. This time her feet seemed to stick to the asphalt. Her knees bent for a moment in a position of prayer and then she was lying on her back, hands still straining to remove her own neck, legs wide open.

The eyes shifted now, with her whole womanhood open for display. They didn't mind what emotions were laid bare, what fears exhibited, what brutality shown, but the physical exposure moved their eyes, shocked them round corners, behind hands. For one flashing moment they were shamed, shamed with the knowledge that this was where they came from, shamed in memory of their own mothers, sisters, daughters, selves.

She was lying across the middle of the road, legs as if in stirrups, pushing her pelvis off the ground, hands still tearing her neck apart. And no one, no one moved to stop her.

This was madness. No one would touch it. But it touched them. So they laughed and walked over to pausing cars or latecomers to tell them the story from the beginning, enjoying being the talebearer, decorating their story with choice superlatives.

Then, as suddenly as it had started, it stopped. She collapsed into stillness in the middle of the road.

They felt cheated. Not now when we are gathered, not now without a grand finale, a special surprise, something to be passed on for generations. It didn't matter that some had gone to school with her, others to church, some sharing the same yard in days gone by. It didn't matter that someone must have loved her or at least, lain with her. No one here found a strand by which to raise her. She was now, untouchable.

'Smaddy move her nuh,' shouted a bus driver from the safety of his cab, thoughts now turned to any profits from a Christmas morning run.

'Why you nuh dweet?' came the reply from somewhere off the road.

'Wah do her? She nuh know is Christmas, she tink is Good Friday?'

It took two strangers, a passing American tourist on a bike with a dread, riding pillion. The first had been through Vietnam, had collected comrades in serious states and hugged them back to life. The second, knowing what it was to be an outcast, with a little arrogance to his step, was going to show them that Jah despised no one.

They moved towards her but, before they could touch her, she rose, gracefully, a dancer rising from her closing position to take her curtain call and then, at the last moment, ignored the audience. She moved with awesome beauty to her step, off the road, onto the beach and walked into the water.

Everyone rushed to the sandy edge. She was going to drown herself. She was already a way out into the water and no one was going to get their clothes wet. They had to see death raise its face before a helping hand would move and, even then, there would be hesitation, for stronger in them was a callous thirst, a deep and twisted agony, slaked only by destruction. This, married to an unreasonable hope for miracles held them, ummoving, on the sandy edge.

The sun and water shone off her and she seemed like the first and only living thing to have walked the waters.

Three times she leaned her head back into the water and rose again, a shaft of light held round her, three times. And then, she cupped her hands and lifted them carefully out of the water.

The watching eyes saw the shape of something small fly away.

Only she only knew that it had been a drowning firefly. It had led her from the tree in the hills where she had been about to hang herself that morning, and she had heard it drowning.

She watched it fly, her head lifted to heaven, silver drops of water falling softly round her...and she smiled...

'Dem never want yuh here...ah never mean to betray yuh but...dem never want yuh here...an dem waiting fi yuh again ...wen ah kiss yuh...ah was only trying to warn yuh...yuh see...ah love yuh Jesas...ah really love yuh...'

She walked out of the water, through the midst of them, untouched. She was singing, 'free at laas...free at laas...'

No one moved towards her. No one could.

And no one laughed. For there, on the beach behind her, appeared a rope, like a hangman's noose. And it had been chewed open.

mansong

lovin he
   was
carryin
   water
in
   basket
ova a
   parch lan

parch
   im drink
an drink
   im parch
again

Porty

The village just woke up one morning and he was there. Him and a beaten up canoe called 'Lover Girl 16'. God only knows what had happened to the fifteen before.

When I saw him, he was removing bits of cardboard from her bottom and beginning to build himself a home, right there on the beach.

Well. I mean. People thought it was funny for a while and watched him from their constant seats on the logs beside the sea wall. In fact, it was a good thing that he had come; hadn't been any amusement in the village for a while. There were quite a few televisions in the homes now, but constant power cuts frequently damaged the equipment and, anyway, it only came on in the evenings. The days were long and slow and the heat only seemed to slow them down some more. At least by the sea there was always a cool breeze.

Now, no one is sure how he came to be called Porty. Some say it was because he came from Portland, others say he was on his way to Portland. One thing is sure, they didn't learn it from Porty because he didn't talk to anyone. Not that he was rude and aggressive, or even dumb, because he had been heard singing, but as far as people were concerned, he had nothing to say.

All day he chewed a home-made cigar which he never lit, and with bits of wire, zinc and bamboo, scrounged along the beach, built what finally emerged as a fish pot. Not like any fish pot that had ever been seen in the village, but when he put in into his canoe one day and took it out to sea, as all the local fishermen did with theirs, everyone knew it was meant to be a fish pot. The amazing thing was that, little by little, Porty's canoe was bringing in fish. At first, not enough to sell, but enough to stop the laughing of the villagers on the logs. Then, as the catch increased, a few enterprising women, with empty enough pots, would make their way to his boat. This caused a new stir of interest as Porty repeatedly shook his head to the crumpled bills they offered, and then, one day, pointed to a woman's basket of freshly drawn red peas. The laughter this trade brought was like a bellyful to the watchers that day, but flavoured with a little respect.

After a few weeks, the entertainment provided by Porty was beginning to wear off, and faces turned again to the sea, the sky and the setting rain.

Until one morning. The lumbering Field Marshall bus that travelled the length of the island once a day, because it needed all day to do it, stopped on the beach road to the cries of the watchers 'One more gear driver'. The driver gladly obliged, showing his skill with gear box and stick. Then he sounded the horns in his usual style, '*pa pa pa pah pa pah*', usually translated as, 'a pretty gal yuh want!'

All the eyes watched the powerfully built woman who stepped down. The village had seen strong women before, indeed, had its fair share, but this woman was tall and had arms and legs that could row a boat three times the size of the local canoes.

She laid down her basket on the sea wall, took off her straw hat to reveal thick plaits pinned across her head, and fanned herself for a while. Then she turned, looking slowly from the hills round to the seaside, nodding to herself as if to say, *yes, this looks like the kind of place*. She signalled to the driver who moved off slowly with his panting bus, stretching his gears into the last possibility of a scream before easing into a change. Picking up her basket, she stepped over the wall and walked along the beach, reading the names of the boats. *Primrose, Set Sail, Satta Massa, Dinah O*... 'Ah', the sound escaped her, '*Lover Girl 16*.'

Her voice was louder than the jukebox, even when it was turned up on a Saturday night.

'Sixteen! Sixteen! Imagine, sixteen time now, yuh mek me have to pack up bag and baggage an come traipsing halfway round dis likkle piece a rock dat drop off a God han eena de sea wen Im carrying de res a de eart go put dung eena it righ-ful place! Sixteen! Well Nicodemus, yuh countin betta dan me, but ah going to lick number an all out a yuh head once an for all, an ah hope yuh don't find no idiot gal in dis place

dat would wutless enuff fi come lie dung wid yuh pon card-
board, fah wen me done wid her she will be good fah nutting
but fish feeding.'

By this time, Porty, who like any self-respecting, early ris-
ing fisherman, was taking his midday nap, had struggled out
of his cardboard hut, almost lifting it off the ground with him
in his haste.

She almost lifted him off the ground, depositing him by the
sea wall. 'Yuh stay right here, an don't say a word.'

At this, laughter broke out from the log where a fair sized
group of villagers were now gathered. She bent to look into
the hut, having to lean quite a bit. For a moment she seemed
like a rock worn down by sea. An instant later, her head re-
emerged with a satisfied, 'huh', and leaving Porty, or Nico-
demus, as he was now known, frozen by the wall, she set to
work.

Finding two long pieces of stick, she rammed them into
crabholes using more sand to make them firm. She then took
some wire in a coil from her basket, and attached it to both
posts to resemble some sort of a clothes line. Without turning
to look at Nicodemus, she asked, 'Weh de fish yuh ketch dis
mawning?'

He pointed out two dismal looking goat fish, already scaled
and drying on a banana leaf. Her grunt told us everything
she thought of him as a fisherman. Her eyes moved to the
two yams near the hut. 'At least, yuh remember someting
dat ah teach yuh.'

She hung the fish on the line, swiping at a fly whom, we were
all sure, would not dare to enter her premises again. Then
she dug into the basket, pulled out some clothing, bent and
forced her way into the hut which could now be seen moving,
from outside.

What was big enough for Porty was not big enough for this
woman. She emerged in what we gathered were her yard
clothes and hung the dress she had been wearing on the other
side of the line from the fish. Turning briskly, she walked to
Porty's fireside and deftly, with bits of dry wood, made a fire,
putting the fish and the yam to roast. Then, hands akimbo,

she stood, surveying the sea. For her, the watching villagers did not exist. Anyone who had nothing better to do than watch other people work were not worthy of notice in her book.

'Weh de standpipe?'

He pointed down past the sea wall, just round a corner. Without hesitation, she reached back into the hut and grabbed some old torn khaki which we recognised as Porty's change of clothes and marched off towards the pipe with the words, 'mek sure de food nuh burn'! Taking a few steps, she turned, 'an don't badda to move; yuh should know by now dat it just don't mek no sense.'

But we had never seen Porty move so quick. As she rounded the corner and bent to turn on the pipe, he was loosing the rope holding the boat to a sea-grape tree. Then, seeming to take a chance, he took the stick from his tin of tar and hurriedly changed the number six to seven. Then he was in the boat, pulling the oars with a passion and taking off for sea.

The village was cracking up with laughter. Some of us pulled out pieces of cardboard from the hut and, wading into the water, threw them into his boat. He never said a word, just nodded.

The woman, on hearing the loud laughter, came running back up the beach, shouting.

'Nicodemus, yuh know dere is nowhere yuh can lan on dis island dat ah cyaan find yuh. An wat yuh going to do widdout a change of clothes, yuh never move so fast as to leave yuh clothes an yuh hut before. Nicodemus!'

She was now by the water's edge.

'Nicodemus, dat is nat fair, yuh know ah cyaan swim! Nicodemus!'

But there was no sign of the boat turning. The whole village stood now, watching the woman, awaiting the storm.

It broke so quietly, they nearly missed it. She stood, looking at the boat, her fear of water showing in the way she avoided the wash of the waves. Then she lifted the hem of her dress and wiped what could only have been a tear. Turning slowly she walked to the fireside. Pulling the food out, she wrapped it carefully. She took down the line, repacking her basket, putting the half damp clothes and the food on top. Then she folded up what was left of the cardboard and tied them together with the wire. Ready at last, she climbed back on the road. Looking at no one in particular, she spoke.

'Is time to settle down, yuh know, cyaan keep running roun de islan like dis. Is nat a good way to start a family, an man shouldn't married unless im inten to start a family.

Then, looking up at the sun to check the time, she moved off slowly in the direction the canoe had gone...land, in pursuit of sea.

Still, she knew, we all knew, a canoe couldn't stay at sea forever and who, in dem right mind, would want to row to Cuba?

packing

i
    walkin out dis place
            nice an easy
packin mi bag neat
            beatin a
                    slow retreat
doan have no
            property to protec
                    no workers to neglec
                            no politician fren
                                    no drugs man weh a go len
mi a fortune
i
    cyaan kill de battyman
        or sell out to foreign plan
            nor kiss no govament ass
                jus waan get aff de crass
name decency
                    so
i
    walkin out dis place
        nice an easy
            no qualms

today

de sky ovacaas but
nat wid mercy
de rosary bead dem wear dung
yet de numbers nah change
how lang man? how lang before
we tap kin puppa lick
an bruk like fever grass?

how lang before
we tek de lang tail jankrow
by de ass
an today downtradden people
get de ovapass?

Sunday Cricket

Look man, is a hard ting wen is Easter Sunday, West Indies battin, an yuh wife decide dat de whole family have to go to church. Nat only de West Indies battin, but dey look like dey set to win de series. Englan go one up in de firs tes, de secon wash out, de third we scrape troo wid a draw by de grace of God rain. I say God save Englan so often dat is high time likkle blessing fall pon we. De fourth, we win, wid a much questioned wicket wen dem say Richards pressure de umpire. Doah I watch it, I cyaan really say wedda de man out or not, I is nat im bat so I cyaan say wat touch mi, but ah do know dat de umpire was already walkin away from behin de stumps as it was de end of de over, wen Richards run dung pon im an im half turn back an raise de finger. An yuh should see Ambrose face, im nuh so hard yet dat im face doan show surprise an doubt no matter wat im body appealin for.

Well dat gone. We win, but nat wid no sweetness fi me. Dis laas tes now, dis is serious business. Yes, we all have a betta feeling fi de England team since dem get rid a de racis dem an even have tree West Indian pon dem side. Despite all dis doah, we still can't lose we pride so much as to mek Englan beat we.

All dat aside, today is de third day a de laas test an bwoy, we battin sweet. Englan all out fi 260 an Haynes an Greenidge nearly pass dat. Nat a man nat out, imagine, an yuh wife insisting yuh have to go to church because is Easter Sunday.

Now yuh probably wonderin why I tek up Bredda B case so, but bein a woman who love her cricket, is a dilemma I well understan. Bredda B is mi neares neighbour an is him I get a answerin moan from wen a fella out or a joyful shout wen ah holla cross, 'Bredda B, yuh see dat cover drive!' Add to dat de fac dat I promise my madda sincerely to accompany her to church dat very same Sunday. I mek dat promise long before I know de date dem fi di game an she wearin a look pon her face dat say life goin to be well miserable for a lang time if ah change mi mind. Nothin like bein comrades in suf-ferin to create a likkle sympaty.

De final woe of de mawnin never befall we until, in we own separate house, we each tryin to find de earplug fi we transistor radio. Sister B mussi did know wat Bredda B was plannin because all de corner dem dat im would usually put de ear plug dat would change de radio into a walkman was well empty. As to me, it was jus caylissniss.

We was two sorry an dutiful people as we set aff to church dat mawnin, already a few minutes late. At de laas moment ah decide to push de likkle radio in mi bag anyway. Ah don't say a ting to Bredda B as im might go smile too broad an mek im wife suspicious. We reach, an tek we usual seat in de back bench while my madda an im wife head towards de choir.

Well bwoy, de firs ting get we vex is wen we see who come out to lead de service. Now, we was sure it had to be Pastor or some visiting dignitary fi dis special day, but nuh same ole Bredda Kelly who we all know since we goin to Sunday school. To put it to de bes compliment we can find, de man is barely literate. Im can read yes, but de way im string im words together an de lengt a time im tek to figure out de nex one, we done lose all sense about wat gone before. Yuh all know how bible haad fi mek sense of already. Nat to mention, dem set a mike in de pulpit, but im so short nat even im breat can ketch it, so we dung a back can hardly hear a ting.

Now if Bredda Kelly did have a bit of drama to im, yuh know, a likkle grunt here or dere like im in pain or a hop skip an jump an den pounce dung hard pon de bible, it would did keep we more activated. But Bredda Kelly, im talk like im constipated.

I grimacin to myself doah Bredda B tekkin it all in stride. Dat only mean dat since de bes course nuh wan possible an de secondary course a wash out, im tek de third course which was, im resort to sleep. Im head was back pon de bench an im mout wide open.

I dere, itchin fi di radio, but tryin to tek Bredda Kelly wid more patience dan God give Job. Yuh see, ah have reason to believe is I who cause it.

I don't really come to church every Sunday, but Pastor an I talk frank. Ah was active as a teenager but yuh all know dat

dat is wen de affairs of de worl get really interesting. But dat is anadda story. However, since ah come home dis time from my wanderins, Pastor aks mi if ah wouldn like to tek up mi membership again. Ah had to explain dat if ah should tek dat course of action ah would lose out on mi ministry wid de yout in particular since right now ah could sit down an have a real progressive an spiritual discussion about every subjec under de sun wedda dem was drinkin a likkle rum or smokin some good bush.

To give Pastor full justice, im see de point an did admit dat de church get really conservative an if im was to practise de ministry like Jesus, de very member dem would criticise. Im aks mi if ah was comin to church de nex Sunday, which wasn't no special day, an ah tell im ah only comin if is im preachin but ah really nat goin to sit down an listen to some sleepy borin member who lackin in any kine of inspiration. I don't feel dat de number of years yuh spen in church qualify yuh to preach. I believe in callin, an who call to tek up collection or repair de bench is nat necessarily who call upon to preach de word of God. Pastor never agree wid dat; im say is de word important, nat who preachin it.

So wen I see Bredda Kelly tek de pulpit, ah say to miself, bwoy, Pastor pull a faas one to teach mi a likkle humility. Dat would mek mi laugh on anadda day for ah enjoy Pastor sense a humour, but nat on a Sunday wen ah give up some brilliant stroke play in wat look like a record breakin openin paatnership an a winnin West Indies team.

So dere we was, de backbenchers, one sleepin, one bored, an Bredda Kelly ramblin on in between de song dem dat always start too high fi my medium key voice. Ah couldn't help feelin dat de spirit in Recreation Groun in Antigua mus be a lot more suitable to de idea of de risen Lord dan de feelin in dis church. Dis feelin more like Good Friday.

It was right in de middle of dat thought dat Bredda B let out a loud half cut off snore an mi see im wife eye searchin im out. Jus as de choir singin 'up from de grave he arose', Bredda B voice ring out, loud an clear, 'dem drop im, man, im get a life!'

Yuh should see Sista B face swell up, an as to how she red already. De whole set a young people side a we bus out wid laugh an den ketch demself quick an push dem yeye back eena dem hymnbook. Bredda B don't know a ting, im head jus rock to de adda side an im silent again. Bredda Kelly cyaan do more dan gwaan wid de service.

I feel so relieve wen I hear Bredda Kelly announce dat is nat him preachin de sermon, is Bredda Jerry. Now Bredda Jerry have nuff energy an can guarantee fi wake up de people dem, plus, im use to play cricket nuff before im meet de Lord an have to give up im Sunday. Well, im tek de pulpit an tings staat to heat up. Immediately im call a chorus an han start clap an cymbal soun up.

Dis is a fairly new ting in Baptis church. Troo de older generation of de membership is fram a likkle higher up de social order, dem use to show dem status by refusin to clap han an play cymbal. Dat did leave to de Pentecostal dem where de poorer people go. It seem to me dat troo dem did only have few member lef who was all ready to move on to heaven, dem decide fi lively up wid some riddim an try bring een some young people. It workin too.

Church staat swing. Bredda Jerry get een pon im sermon an even Bredda B staat rock likkle bit eena im sleep, open one eye an drif aff again wid a timely 'Amen'.

Wen Bredda Jerry reach de risen Lord now, im tell de whole church fi stan up an say, 'Praise de Lord'. De church shout 'Praise de Lord'. Bredda Jerry say 'Wave yuh han in de air an say Tank yuh Jesas'. De church raise dem han an say 'Tank yuh Jesas'. Bredda Jerry say 'Yes, yes, bredrin an sistrin, we have a saviour. It is nat de empty grave dat is important today, dat could have been a samfie man trick, a Nansi game. What is important today is de Risen Lord, de Risen Lord. He is our hero an He is here. Mek we clap we han an give a roun of applause to de Risen Lord.'

De whole church give a firm an loud clap han. Is dis rise Bredda B, im jump up quick, like im late fi heaven, clappin im han an hollerin out 'Im mek a double century or im out?'

As soon as dis come out im mout, de laughin bus out fresh

from de back an de vex face dem turn roun from de front.
Sista B put dung her hymnbook an staat head out troo de side
door so she can come een troo de back door fi im. My madda
face tight like no joke cyaan mek fi at leas a year.

Is Bredda Jerry save de day, ah have to give it to dat man.
Im answer Bredda B right back. 'Out? Out? Nooooo...Not
out, never out. We have a openin bat dat never out. None
like Him been aroun for centuries. An church, if yuh have
Him on yuh side yuh cyaan lose, no, yuh cyaan lose. My
openin bat, your openin bat. Mek Im lead dis team today.
Jesus! What is His name?...Jesus! Caall on His name...'

De whole congregation bawl out, 'Jesus'. All de backbencher
dem come een, 'Jesus'.

Bredda B, wide awake now, breathe out in sheer relief as
im wife stop at de doorway an head back to de choir jus as
Bredda Jerry raise de final song.

> *Up from de grave He arose*
> *wid a mighty triumph o'er His foes*
> *He arose a victor from de dark domain*
> *An will live forever wid de saints to reign.*

We voice lif up like we was ready to over run a pitch.

> *He arose He arose*
> *Hallellujah, Christ arose.*

Me an Bredda B let out a sigh of relief an we really did
mean dat final 'Amen' fah we know how often we go dung
into terror wid we cricket, collapse afta a good start into de
grave, but we always rise again, hallellujah, always to rise
again!

Song for Lara

is a young generation
comin dung sweet
nat in awe of *Wisden*
nat studyin defeat

a fresh clean page
from an islan of dreams
a bat in han an
burstin at de seams

de wicket holds no shadows
of what cannot be reached
Jus
practisin, dread,
gettin better all de time
de limelight doan mean nutten
wid a bat in mi han
liftin up mi head
an thinkin bout de glory
is a sure way to be out
before de en a de story

if de bowler fine a reason
ah will answer wid a rhyme
any kine a riddim
in mi own time

                  Pan man, hole tight.

Lara een
im tekkin up im guard
fus one straight back
dung de pitch
Dis is between we an de Lord!

We bus out a heaven gate today
wid a certain majesty
buil a hero to open space
from all dat crampin' we

lightnin flash troo de covers
breakin de boundary
den we sekkle back pon de riddim wid a
Nooooo...defensively

Dance it, Lara, dance it
de march deh pon we foot
steady timin
watchful eye
wait for de tenor pan
to fly
lash it
cause it overpitch
bruk a man han
if im try ketch it
is a four, is a six, is a sure ticket
anyting ah have, Lawd,
ah gamble it

dem slow dung de riddim now, mi son,
so steady timin, bassman, come!
deh sayin we don't like it slow
deh call we calypso cricketers
say we cyaan hole dung tempo
so we sen for David Rudder now
is a ballad in kaiso
so slow...so slow
a ballad in kaiso

> *'Come mek we rally...y...y...y*
> *rally rung de West Indies'*

an wen we wear dem dung again
we gawn forward extempo

is a pair a eye dat see de ball
before de bowler   tink it

a pair a leg dat dance wid ease
anywhere he   lan it

a pair a han dat have more joint
dan jus elbow   an wris

is a fella dat will fine de gap
instead a mindin it
instead a mindin it

an all de time
he smilin sweet
gentle, humble
dress well neat
bat like a ratchet
in he han
slicin troo
de hard red heat

    an he playin hiself
      he playin hiself
but he doan play all hiself yet

    he playin hiself
      he playin hiself
but he doan play all hiself

yet

caribbean woman

oh, man,
oh, man,
de caribbean woman

oh, man,
oh. man,
de caribbean woman

she doan fraid a de marchin beat
she doan care how he timin sweet
she doan care if she   kill a man
jus doan mash up she plan

caribbean woman does
cry
like rain a sprinkle
early friday mawnin
does
bawl like tundastorm
late satday night

doan have no special time
fi wash she eye

caribbean woman does
kick she man out
in de black a nite
wen er eye meet im guilt
wid a moonblood red
dat mek im feel like a dawg

but she does
welcome she man
somedays later
wen she fine she have a

certain itchin
dat no odder finger can scratch

caribbean woman does
rise she son
 wid a drumbeat pon im back
 fi fine im ancestry
 den spoil he
 fi fine he wife

 she does rise she daughter
 pon a mountain range a breas
 bringin de sweetes milk
 same time she

  cookin
  washin
  ironin

same time she

  cussin
  winin
  jokin

same time she

  prayin
  'oh, lawd'

 an wen yuh see she
 walk

wen yuh see
caribbean woman walk

on she lef
de cliff
to san
to sea mare
wavin wid er flow
de deep belly laughter slap
of water
gains she rock

        an on she right
        de blue mountain peak
        she does force yuh to reach
        if yuh seekin travel
        troo er ferny green
        er cocoa smell
        er coffee mawnings
        aaah

wen yuh see she walk

    holdin freedom water

    balance pon she head

    an de hips
    de hips dat hole de sway
    to a tousan hallellujahs

    an de breas
    dat point de way
    troo no man's lan
    dat lan she know so well
    yet
    never stap for long

    wen yuh see she walk
    yes
    wen yuh see she

den yuh fine grace
bwoy

is den yuh fine yuh grace

        oh, man,
        oh, man,
        de caribbean woman

        oh, man,
        oh, man,
        de caribbean woman

        she doan fraid a de marchin beat
        she doan care if he timin sweet
        she doan care if she   kill a man
        jus doan mash up she plan

        jus doan mash up she plan

Kitchen Talk

From I know Nathan, im been a fool wid money. De firs samfie man dat ketch im gawn wid all im have an Nathan still dere tinkin is him owe de man. Dat is Nathan.

Mark yuh, im have im good ways as a man. Im never speak disrespectful to me, an if im have nuff woman im keep dem far. I doan watch im. All dese years I never aks Nathan where he going to or where he coming from, an to tell yuh de truth, he never aks me.

Nathan love im rum, yes. An if im don't want to put on shirt an tie to go to church on Sunday, dat is Nathan business. God didn't mek me responsible fi no man soul, no matter wat parson say. No amount a sermon about who livin wid who in sin an who mus be missionary in dem own house going to mek me start get miserable in here. Dis is my kingdom an ah sure de Lawd doan vex dat ah carve out mi own likkle place an run it to de bes a mi ability. So Nathan can do what he doin.

Yuh big now, an ah talkin to yuh woman to woman. Yuh cannot change man. If dat is wat yuh tryin to do wid Peter, yuh can forget it.

When I meet Nathan, I done know Nathan. Ah know Nathan granfadda, im madda, im sista. I grow up near Nathan breed, an if yuh know de breedin, yuh can have a good idea of how smaddy goin to turn out. Dat is nat to do wid riches, dat is to do wid how dem brought up.

Yuh see Miss Icy children. Dat man don't give er a cent. Seven pickney, same man, an nutting to depend on. I see Icy tek een all kine a work an bring up dem children clean an neat. Icy did have a one room wood house an she teach dem children fi live good togedda an see all a dem come out come tek to dem book an mek someting of dem life. Dat is de pride dat Icy put in dem. An see de man. Im still a draw im tear up trousis out a street. Yuh can imagine if she did meet a decent man dat did know imself.

Dat is why I doan complain bout Nathan. Ah tell im, from de start. Ah say 'Nathan, yuh can tek dat big ting yuh have in yuh trousis an go an push it anyway yuh choose, but de day I feel one likkle scratchin under me like yuh bring home no disease, is de laas time yuh allow into my privacy.

An all de time I sayin dis, I know is which man I talkin to. I don't jus talk so, for man is different. Some of dem doan have no self respec, but Nathan, im was always a man wid pride. Is de kine a man dat like to know im have a secret place somewhere dat only im one get permission to visit. Yes. An I know how to please Nathan, dat's a woman sweetness, but yuh mus know dat by now from de size a dat belly in front a yuh.

Pass a cup a water mek ah rub up two dumplin. All a Nathan tribe love dumplin in dem soup. Is dem yuh bredda tek after.

So what yuh really tellin mi now, yuh frettin bout Peter keepin woman. You pregnant up dere in Peter big house an im nat comin home till mawnin. Is wat yuh want from mi, sympaty. Ah tell yuh wen yuh meet Peter firs an gettin all giddy bout im, ah tell yuh, keep di likkle job dung a Water Commission an keep on goin to evenin school so yuh can upgrade yuh station. Ah never tell yuh dat! All dem days ah sayin, save up an buy a bed. At leas mek sure yuh own de bed. Now yuh lyin dung wid Peter big belly, in Peter big bed, in Peter big house, wid no Peter?

Baby is nat a ting to keep man at home, yuh done know dat already. Mos time dem frettin in case yuh fine out how similar dem an de baby is in dem behaviour. But I know what wrong wid yuh every part a yuh full up wid Peter. Yuh figet yuh name Evadne? Yuh figet yuh is mi daughter? I is a woman no man ever ketch out so. Ah did tell yuh, at leas own de bed, keep di job. But no. Peter doan want im woman to work. Peter like to see yuh dere wen im get een. Peter like im dinner hot on de table. Peter say im earnin enough to support we. Peter say is only me one can iron im shirt how im like it. Peter say...Peter say...Peter say...An where was Evadne all dis time? Where is Evadne now? Pack up de job dat could give yuh any sense a freedom. Can't even buy a panty if yuh doan aks Peter. Well...never in me, my madda or my granmadda generation, I ever see a galpickney born dat doan have no pride in ownin she own tings.

Yuh see dat savins book I have up at de Post Office? Yuh tink Nathan name on it? Yuh tink Nathan can draw no money out of it? No, mamma, my life doan go so.

Ah doan say Nathan doan work, but Nathan fool wid money. It run in im tribe. Im granfadda use to own all a dat pasture lan yuh see over Spence Pen. Gamble an drink rum till im lose de whole ting. Im fadda use to have a good qualify job, nice house, im run lef im wife an mek stray gal nyam out every cent out a im. Dat is how come Nathan en up wid nutten, an Nathan was headin down de same road. Im use to have all de fren in de world jus because dem could depen on im to buy de nex flask a rum. If I never pluck im out a dere, im look like any odder wreck of a man yuh see walkin dung de road today.

An Nathan know dat. Im know im place is here, so is fi him job fi find it. I nat going out dere to look for Nathan, an if im mek one wrong move dat give anybody in dis district any cause to call my name wid disrespec, im foot cannot pass dis gate, because ah put de house in my name to.

Ah tell oonu from young, you an yuh sister Barbara, ah say, doan tun fool fi man. Love dem all yuh want, but doan tun fool fi dem. Mos man jus a learn, dem doan come to de realities a life yet. Is nat dat we born any wiser, but we did always have to face up to de responsibility a we action, so we know how to run tings, how to mek a likkle bit stretch, mek two ends meet. We know what is priority an what can wait, an we have to tink in de long term for once yuh have a baby, is a whole life time dat yuh have in sight.

Man don't want dem kine a insight or foresight. Dem wi like fi see dat de baby resemble dem, walk it out one evenin pass de football match, if is a bwoy, jus to show everyone dat dem vital parts still functionin, but after dat dem is helpless. If dem do want to prove say dem is de fadda, dem come een an want to discipline everybody. Dat is a ting me never allow. You tink me could bruk my body in two fi have a chile, wuk hard fi feed it, everyday, sick or healty, to be dere for it, an wen is time to say 'don't do dat' or 'behave yuhself', I goin to have to call a man? Like I don't have no power over mi own household? No sar, nat even to help im feel like im is a man.

De meat an de peas cook now. Look yuh see a piece a yellow yam under de table. Pass it...an de big cookin knife. But wait, troo de cutex pon yuh finger yuh fraid fi hol de yam? Ah bet yuh dat red lipstick pon yuh mout nat gwine stap yuh from eatin it! Tank yuh mam.

I tell Nathan, yuh know, wen dem bwoy start laugh after im troo dem cyaan drink out im money no more, ah tell im straight. Dem laugh after im an say im mek woman rule im an im mus prove say im is de man. Well, im come in here brave up pon rum one evenin to tell mi, dat is after im eat de dinner done yuh know, to tell mi dat is im wear de trousis in de house an I mus stop behavin like I is a man.

I tell Nathan den an dere. I strip off all mi clothes, ah was four months pregnant an de belly jus stan up, ah tell Nathan, naked, ah say, Nathan is only wen yuh tek off yuh clothes an come into dis bed dat I want to know what a man is...for I know what woman is...but wen it come to outside dere wid all de tings to be done, everybody born wid two han an everybody born wid common sense...yuh done know say yuh life well suit yuh, so if you want to follow dem bwoy out a street always runnin from one woman to de odder, den tek all yuh manness an gwaan. Dat's wat I tell Nathan. An ah wasn' goin to break mi heart if im walk out de door dere an den, baby or no baby. Well, as yuh can see, im is still here, an im might not know it, but im is more of a man fi dat. Im even get a lot more pleasin in bed!

Wat you lookin so shocked about? Yuh tink yuh madda too ole fi dem tings, or she shouldn't talk about dem? You young, you tink pleasure is your perrogative, but wen you have dat baby, yuh will begin to know a few more tings, especially bout man.

one last dub

dis is one time dat de
message laas
to de constant bubblin
      of de riddim below
      de waisline
fah people packet did lang time
      absalete
cep fi few crumbs   cockroach
      couldn't reach
      so if yuh could jus tease
      mi wid a riddim
fi fling up wi distress   eena
      dance hall style
      fah eberyting   still runnin
wile
before de shat let aff
mek we   bruk
          in dis likkle corner
          wid we back
          tight
          agains de wall
            Lawd!
ah should go to church
tomorrow
      but ah want de harves happen right
      eena mi own yaad
an Gad know
to how de pot empty a ile
mutten wouldn't spwile
but   fah tinite, sweet jesas,
        ah gwine let go to de pulsin beat
        below de belt
        is where de shitstim hit we
        all de time
        truut is truut

                        an nuff fly bus a dance
but baas
no ride no haas craas
                        we hold de whip
                        we hold de beat
                        right yah so
                        which paat yuh put it

an riddim nuh partial, baas,
no
riddim no partial

The Last Temptation

She had to walk it this time.

She had arrived in his car from the neighbouring village and, for the last year and a half, she had sat like a queen in the front seat, on her way to another shopping, another fun day on the beach, another night out at a dance or the movies. She had waved to the chosen few, but never stopped to talk, because she never walked. He had liked it that way. His woman shouldn't be too local, shouldn't be caught up in any gossip, should be only his.

And so she would have to walk it, this first and last time, walk before their naked eyes. She knew they were waiting. She knew they knew.

Purposefully putting a bit more swing into her full bottom, she walked, the suitcase in her hand, towards the bus stop. All the eyes followed her as she went past, bold country stares that took in even the colour of thread that seamed her dress. But she could handle the eyes of women, so she swung her hips a bit more to be sure they got their fill.

As she passed the laughter broke, loud, startling, against the quiet pattern of the waves. She felt the quick anger stir in her bosom. She could turn now and tell them a few colours of choice 'claats', but she would not let herself sink to their level, not now.

Anyway, if she did turn, they would all be studying a surprised crab as if it had just performed a skilled act, better than walking sideways. Yet, they would all know she had turned, proving that their laughter had affected her. She wouldn't give them that satisfaction.

They hadn't been able to laugh before. Had studied her with curiosity, dislike, then open hatred, as she had seen in fleeting glances from the car. But they had stopped at laughing, because her man had hired most of their men and they couldn't take that chance between a full and an empty pot.

Floating behind her, she heard the word 'fool', and to make it worse, he drove past just then in the new Lada, blowing his horn at two goats scratching at stray paper in the road.

He wouldn't look her way. He was too angry. All he could do was speed up with a gear change of pure disdain. She had to smile as the gears crashed. He never did have a gentle touch. Still, she speeded up a little, making sure the suitcase didn't drag her down, for he would pass again soon on his daily taxi run.

She flung her hips and pulled her shoulders even straighter, knowing full well the strength of her body as she moved on down the road. She had seen it reflected from young in the jealous eyes of women and the waiting eyes of their men.

Yes, they could laugh now and call her a fool but she knew, and God knew too, that no man would ever lay a hand on her again, no matter what kind of car he drove, what kind of house he put her in, or how much furniture and clothes he bought. No man was ever going to beat her up one minute and expect to let off his stinking alchoholic juices between her legs in the next. No. Cause she didn't want to maim or kill somebody, and only the next woman he dared to take off his underpants in front of, would ever know how close she'd come.

The wind picked up a voice. It came screeching at her, high and righteous.

'Mule, de man haffi kick her out troo she cyaan breed. Er womb mash up since she trow weh di pickney wen she eena primary school.'

Not even the weight of her bosom could stop her this time. She dropped the suitcase and was crossing the bank from the road and back down the beach. The group of women were up, like the feathers on a fowl's back when chickens are disturbed. She didn't even have to ask who. Lulu's voice had that pitch ever since the power cut in the hospital when the doctor was removing her tonsils.

Half of her blouse came away with the first grab. In five minutes, neither of them had a stitch of clothes left on their backs. Only blood and sand, and half the village on the road, laughing and pointing.

She didn't hear the Lada stop, but she knew it was him who

came to part them. And suddenly she knew what had gone wrong. It wasn't Lulu she wanted to beat, it was him.

In one movement, she picked up the ragged stone and, swirling like a discus thrower, lodged it in his head. He went down, flat, and took the whole screaming crowd off her back.

She didn't wait to see, just wrapped what rags were left around her and walked straight to the Police Station, blood pouring from her hands and knees.

That night, sitting in her cell, smoking her last cigarette, she decided it was better to take revenge and go to hell, than ride round dead and decent, with a graveyard as her smell.

Ratoon

it's the eyes that haunt me most

young men
grown old
too quickly

last sugar stick
surrrounded by dry leaves
no water reaches roots

the eyes
forced ripe
and plucked
long before the coming

some deep worm
now growing old
a rubbed out reddening
of old age
with nothing

there are no pensions here
and careless days
in cane passion
don't outlast a dewdrop
in this heat

and the eyes
sunken now
and blinded with
dead dreams

the wind laughs
a dry sound
of parched stones
in the bed

where waters once
cooled desire
smoke rises
out of a chestful
of gravel

one with fire
we perspire
to our loss
clutch the tales
of rags to riches
somewhere
over Lotto's horizon
replant me Lord
and send a visa come

but even that needs youth
to be cut down
and the joints
now withering
spirit burning
flesh done

any growth is singed
by want of rum

asked for one more smiling
to the sun

cane cracks

these eyes cannot lie
about the heart

already
all around
the next ratoon
is coming

old cane eyes
burnt out
watching them
unspeaking

rising in their heat

Return

She was sitting on the verandah steps, skirt wrapped loosely round her knees, head between her legs. She could smell herself, like earth after soft rain. The scent was a natural part of the heat from a cloudless sky on her back, the wind that was teasing, refusing to bring answers, just the passing sound of traffic.

Somewhere round the corner, the radio was crooning another love song. She used to listen to them all night, part of the symphony of crickets, treefrogs, and the moonlight on the coconut trees. Now, in the heat of day, the very perfection made her angry, brought her to silence.

'The problem with you is dat yuh don't know what yuh want...or...yuh want too much. Yuh mus count yuh blessings. Know how much people round yuh don't have a quarter of de chances you get?'

Her mother, having chanced speech, sat back again, still, tight-lipped, afraid of saying too much and sparking an argument. She understood that this daughter would have to go again, somewhere, anywhere, and she wished that she would stop clinging to the idea that she could make any real difference here.

The very beauty would hold her, charm her, and then suck her dry like the cane piece down the road. No. This place didn't have any kindness for soft hearts. Didn't matter how much you could appreciate a rainbow or want to hold a sunset in your palm. This was a beauty you had to have money to appreciate.

Sometimes it was better you didn't educate them so well. What could you do with it in a place like this? Who you going to talk to when you want to find out if is mad yuh mad or just plain discontented?

The mother sighed and put the needle and thread away. She couldn't remember where she had left her glasses, couldn't sew or read much now anyway, constant headaches. Just expecting the light bill or the water rate, or sending to the shop for a few basic necessities and counting out the dollars was enough to cause another pounding in her head. And she didn't have much of a working life left. Still, she had to thank the Lord for the job she had. It had saved the whole family in the worst of times, ever since the government changed a few years back and they had fired her with one month's pay saying she was a socialist. You couldn't do a thing to help anyone in the community any more without them saying you were a political activist. Right now you had to concentrate on your own survival.

She shifted her foot which was getting a cramp from the way she was sitting. A piece of the cover from the verandah chair came away with her as she moved. She would love to change them for Christmas, but it would be enough just to buy food for the household and get a new cylinder of cooking gas. Lord help us, but it would be too much to have to go back to the coal stove with the black dust rising up your nose and sticking to the back of your throat.

The very thought of poverty frightened this mother. She had grown up in the red dirt, scratching for coco and left over yams in other people's fields to help out the family soup pot, and now, thank the Lord, the house was hers and the children had never been hungry. They had been born to different dreams from just being clean and fed. She had a deep fear which only those who had been really poor and escaped could ever understand. And, in this place, the line was so close, it was easy to slip over again into the dirt. No, Lord, please, never again.

She looked back at her daughter. Sometimes it was hard to believe that this was her brightest child, called brilliant in fact, had travelled all over the world performing, but still kept on coming back, still couldn't cut the navel string that held her to this soil. These people would only celebrate her when she was up, but would trample her back into the dust unless they saw round her that golden shine of money.

No. Somehow, she had brought this one up too soft. Things were ruthless now. Not that she herself hadn't been soft too, but years of walking red rockstone, taking people's insults, having to credit flour from the shopkeeper day after day, wearing other children's cast off clothes, had given her a hard core somewhere. She could survive. She had to.

'If I had her chances...she just don't know the chances she getting...'

Her thoughts were interrupted by the loud blaring of horns. They both looked up to see the beginning of a passing political motorcade. People were running out from the yard beside them, voices shouting, as the colourful vehicles passed, like some out-of-place carnival, through the dusty street.

Neither mother nor daughter moved. Like everyone, they had seen it all before, but they knew they had nothing to expect, whatever colour or sign was showing. Thank God they weren't so desperate as to have to follow one or the other, and, as they had never accepted hand-outs, didn't have to pay anyone back with their presence, or perhaps, with their lives.

The grand-daughter ran in from the yard next door where she had been playing, stopping on the steps to grab her mother's hand, pointing excitedly to the road.

'Mommy! Mommy!'

They could see the tall figure of the MP as the motorcade slowed.

'Mommy, ah see de man dat come to listen to yuh readin yuh poems in town. Remember? He was shakin yuh han after and said I was a nice girl. Ah was callin to him an wavin but he didn't see me.'

The daughter-mother smiled, as she always had to when her big-eyed beauty came near her. She opened her legs so the little girl could sit on the lap made by her skirt.

'They wouldn't see us now, darling. They only see you when you're higher up than them. It's hard to look down and recognise people.'

The little girl thought about that for a while. She always had to think for a while about what her mother said, but she loved the sense of mystery in her words and the way she let her into a world of grown up thoughts. She always seemed to be somewhere else, lost in her own daydream, until you did something naughty. She didn't always see but seemed to sense it.

The elder mother looked at them both. The little one looked just like her mother had looked at the same age. Every time she saw them together, something tugged at her belly, a haunting history of the need to better life for her children, a clinging sadness from a land that drained hopes and seriously attacked her faith on lonely nights, a memory of mornings flushed with a dewy beauty when she had to swallow her love whole in time to meet the ever practical sun.

'So when yuh planning to go back to Englan? There's not much for you to do here. If yuh going to be a poet here, yuh have to be a rich poet.'

The daughter-mother held her daughter close, staring out past the now empty street to where there was a shimmer of blue-green sea in the distance.

Both she and her young one knew it would soon be time to part again. She couldn't stand to see her daughter cluttered up in a small flat in the cold of England, not any more than she could clutter herself into a nine-to-five civil service job here. She loved to see her flying through the green hedges to play with neighbouring children, to see her barefoot on the beaches, a little Arawak, watching fishes or climbing trees for fruit. This place was heaven for children if you could feed them well.

Daughter-mother could smell the coming of water and, reaching round, tickled her mother's foot curled on the ground beside her, as she had seen her mother tickle her grandmother's and as her daughter now sometimes tickled hers. This was the only other woman she trusted with her child.

The first drops of rain blessed them as they held.

Somehow, before too many years dreamed by, she was going to find a way home, own a little piece of land with trees and flowers she had planted, build a house where she could live and work. This island couldn't give birth to her, to the voices that she heard inside her head, and then tell her to stillborn them. Sometimes she could feel them, rusting in her chest and sometimes, in rarer moments, she could spit out a pearl, shined up, from hugging herself too tight. But she knew something was dying, slowly, in the cold.

The elder mother lifted herself from the chair as she heard her mother, now old and ill in the same room where her daughter had been born, call out for something to drink.

She looked at her daughter once again, knowing intimately her pain. She had walked that road many years before, leaving her with her grandmother to find some work in town. But somehow, when yuh tink tings should be getting better for the children, this place just seem to get worse and, Lord knows, fresh air good and healthy but it sure mek everybody eat more.

She turned to go in the front door, then tried one last time.

'At least in England dem respec de kine of work yuh do, and she will soon be old enough to join you.'

The afternoon heat lay silently between them.

Somewhere, in the yard, a rooster crowed.

The MP's open vehicle flew past them, running for cover, as the rain came tumbling down.

I Jonah

Ah have to be here, Lawd,
a likkle wile longer

the call came
untimely

I nat ready, Lawd,
is a hard step
cross river Jordan
cross de sea
cross any water

I listening
keen
head still
like a green lizard
on dis trunk a land
not looking for no stone

is de word dat lik mi
in mi head
twis mi
like a serpent
drap mi aff di mountain
into sea

an de whale did
    de whale did
        de whale did
           de res

I Jonah
sayin, Lawd,
doan sen mi dere
I happy here

an de word
comin at mi
over an over again
an de chant rock steady
like so many distant drum

       never get weary yet
       never get weary yet
       down in de valley
       for a very lang time
       never get weary yet

I Jonah
caught up in de miracle
of flight
landin on a distant shore
an word flyin
lef, right, an centre
like a warner woman in de market
writhing with the power
in a breath

but, Lawd,
is nat mi spirit at all
to chant destruction

       touch dem one by one
       gal an bwoy
       dis time a no play we a play
       gal an bwoy
       pointer gawn astray
       gal an bwoy
       which voice hold de sway
       gal an bwoy

I Jonah
used
by a gift of faith
exercised on impulse
spent
retreating
into a babylin hollow
by de sea
back
to an angry mountain
not sure
anymore
which coast is Nineveh